Battlecry

Julie-Ann Booker

BookLeaf Publishing

Presentation by *BookLeaf Publishing*

Web: www.bookleafpub.com

E-mail: info@bookleafpub.com

ISBN: 978-93-95950-46-6

First edition 2022

For my wife, my daughters and my grandchildren - you are the planets of my cosmos

ACKNOWLEDGEMENT

I would like to acknowledge my English teacher Susan Blake, who gave me a love of words.

PREFACE

Words have always jumbled around in my head and I have always found it a pleasant way to spend time trying to put them together in some semblance of order. It always fascinated me that words could be disciplined to carry a story but also go next to each other in rhymes. My mind is like a tangled ball of wool and poetry is like a knitted square, neat and orderly.

Naming the book 'Battlecry' was important because I always felt like my heart had fights with feelings and how other people made me feel. The words draw pictures and capture experiences and some of it is conflict. As the reader, you may feel conflicted about how feelings are depicted, you might feel there is an indulgence, an immersion and that is not necessarily found in respected art, but 'Battlecry' is not for an audience per se, it has been my fight and strategy for survival. There is a naivety in this collection of juvenilia and one day I might be embarrassed by it, but today these are my scars, medals and spent weapons.

Fragile

Why would I be so confused?
Because it is what I deserve.
God knows there is a whip to use
And a punishment yet to serve.
Why would I be so cold?
Because I was scalded before.
God knows I can't get close,
Lest we both drip blood on the floor.

Why was the aim to abuse?
Because it is what I deserve.
God knows we all have to choose
A place which is nearer the nerve.
Why would I be so cruel?
Because pain broke me to the core.
God knows I won't get close.
Lest I pull you down to the floor.

Why would I feel so used?
Because it is what I deserve.
God knows there is so much to lose
And a straight line which we must curve.
Why would I be so calm?
Because rage shook me once more.

God knows I can't let go,
Lest we slip in the red on the floor.

Drowning

Even if you did receive my message could be wrong,
Even if you did believe, belief would not be strong,
And even if you could conceive how much, how far, how long?
Even if you did, you still would not belong.

It was Spring when you first felt her skin on your skin,
The skin that you sleep in and dream of her breathing.

I would lead your horse to the water and I would help you down,
I would wash your face in laughter and I would bathe your frown.
I would see your gaze in mine and find what could be found,
I would feel your love much deeper and I know I would drown.

It was Spring when I first felt your skin on my
skin,
The skin that I sleep in and dream of you
breathing.

Even if I did receive your message could be
wrong,
Even if I did believe, belief would not be strong,
And even if I could conceive how much, how
far, how long?
Even if I did

It was Spring when you first felt my skin on
your skin,
The skin that you sleep in and dream of me
breathing.

Whole

I would build a shelter
Far from feeling this
Where you could not show violence
Of thought or word or fist
Me, untouched and lonely
Would be a silent soul
Bare or clothed, never yours
But absolutely whole

You would not keep a key
You could never be the beast
In here there is no pain
Or vulnerability
Four walls and a window
To look through, to see through, (I see you)
I would not speak and not move
And be invisible

But absolutely whole

R. V. S

I will see the stone is rolled
Let the story just unfold
Heal the skin but break the mould
Karma cannot be controlled

They think I should take denial
When love quells what is hostile
And a shadow on your sun dial
Points to draw me round awhile

How they tried to give me gold
For something that could not be sold
Tried to tell me who to hold
How I should embrace the cold

Ours is not to question why
There is a red velvet sky
The sun murmurs down from high
It is the perfect reply

Come in

"Come in, cumbersome one," you said,
"Kick off your shoes and all your lies,
Give me a second to straighten the bed,
I've been looking forward, look in my eyes."

"Climb inside my mouth now," you said,
"Kick off your blues and close your eyes,
Give me a minute to straighten your head,
I've been getting tired of the same old highs."

"It's all a game, the same," you said,
"You win, you lose and it makes you wise.
Give me a little of your time instead,
Say goodbye to the goodbyes."

Of you

It was back in January,
When you said you wanted to leave me
Didn't June come around soon?
If it's love, then pin on the label
Tell me you feel secure and stable
The point, bursts my thought balloon
Of you

I find your feet still under my table
Get up and walk away if you're able
I'll be waiting for the next moon
Another planet might be more quiet
Far from emotional riot
Where I can sing my lonely tunes
Of you

Your unsettled rock of the cradle
And your loyalty proving a fable
Forgiveness lost and missing
The thing that we hold conflict for
You push war borne of war
Which delivers battle cry kissing
Of you

Now I feel

I was always guilty
Of the sins shown to me
Like not living for what is now
Nature has seen me walking, thinking, talking
Waiting for me to turn around
I know promises spoken are now vows broken
I have been a queen without a crown
I felt so ugly and it flowed all through me

I am never guilty
Of the sins shown to me
I am living for what is now
Nature with me walking, thinking, talking
Waited and I turned around
Now all the promises spoken are no longer
broken
So to the queen her humble crown
Now I feel such beauty and it flows all through
me

Magpie

There's a magpie living in my garden
I remember the day that I fist saw him
It was the day you said you were leaving
It was the day I flew in the sky of freedom

It's black and white, it's blue again
Things look different on reflection
There's no replacing the time that is taken
Just trying to reach that higher feeling

But then the magpie flew away
I was just thinking he might stay
As the colours of the feathers fade
I know I'll never feel this way again

Things look different on reflection
You're somewhere else under the same sun
When you think of me, know I'm trying
Flying towards a new horizon

Book

I run my fingers down your spine
I will turn your pages in time
Throw the book at me
I burn, you burn, when will we learn?

I read your words, I mouth each line
I will feel your lips reading mine
Throw the book at me
But I learn, you learn, tenderly we yearn

I pick you up, I put you down
There on the shelf you won't make a sound
Throw the book at me
But I yearn, you yearn, when will we learn?

Meditation

Appreciate what gratitude could show
Apology is half good and half good to know
Consider letting the river flow
Consideration is a warm undertow

She wonders why those people felled that tree
The tree was only trying to help the people breathe
She can still see the tree's energy
Understanding is breathing carefully

Structure of intention could be good
What was once a should has now changed to would
Illuminate, consider what you should
Illumination is being understood

Ghost

I have to sleep eventually
And when I do I will dream
All the things that dream in me
I don't know what they mean
But if your face filters through
Smiles and shines again
I will wake and cry for you
Keep my eyes open

I have to speak eventually
When I do I will scream
All the things that yell in me
Shout out about the dream
If your voice is in this room
Your words give silence strength
I won't say what I assume
Not speak at any length

I have to learn eventually
When I do I will see
Of all the things that live in me
You are the ghost I need

She

She reflects the sun
Her compassion will make you one
When your work is done
She will be there when you come home
She will be the one
The light that helps you move along

She will play your game
Because it's all done in your name
She will save your day
Because she knows a better way
She will have you sway
She always finds the words to say

She said

She said "Never let the darkness win."
She's watching a changing expression, watching.
She said "Never must you fade within."
She's waiting for the words to sink in, waiting.

She said "Never feel this way again."
She's turning this lesson outside in, turning.
She said "This is spoken, this is said."
She said she understood the meaning, she said.

No

You rationalise all your problems by putting the blame on me.
So, you defend your self-respect and cool integrity,
But I didn't come to get walked upon, used, abused or lose.
I'm happy to see the war is one and I have no enemy.

I suffer your lies and anger rise, I am loaded with constancy.
So, you don't have to carry this, the weight all falls on me,
But I am not yours to be target for the strong arm of your law
I am happy to see the weak will gone and I have the strength to be

No enemy.

Hell, yes

I know you understand this,
Pay attention.
You broke me with a kiss,
A warm interruption.

Did I want it? Hell, yes,
Wanted completion.
No more, no less,
All inclination.

Your tight little stitches,
Came undone.
I see the broken harness,
It is no illusion.

Did I get it? Hell, yes
The train you were on
No way I can escape
A to B with no station

When we fall to madness
Show no relation
To where we feel weakness
Like desperation

Believe

I believe in divine intervention
I was out in the hard rain just moving
Soaked to the skin with crying with trying for
my soul
I didn't even know about knowing
She looked at my face
I believe in divine intervention

I've been stretching a pure living
Iv'e been wishing it didn't sting
I've been holding my arms out in
All the searching I have been doing

I believe in divine intervention
I was out in the sunshine this morning
A rainbow bridged a feeling reviving my soul
I didn't need to know one thing about one thing
She changed my face
I believe in divine intervention

I've been looking for sweet heaven
I've been waiting beneath this skin
I've been hoping someone would get in
I've been praying for this woman

Fair

You didn't even know what you were waiting for
Would it be fair weather?
Tomorrow always knocks you out before you
can get up
To help each other
Tried to bring the fight out of the shadows
Black and blue but the mood smothers
I am sometimes warm
I am sometimes your lover

You didn't even know what you were crying for
It isn't fair is it?
Sorrow washes over you like an ocean
You've got to swim for it
When you put your heart back in the place
That it once knew it's a unique fit
I am sometimes safe
Sometimes you sit where I sit

You didn't even know what you were dying for
Which isn't fair, ever
You borrowed your moments from a wrinkle in
time
You always were clever
But if you put the clock back on itself

You have to catch up forever
I am sometimes near
We should be together

Shine

Your gaze does not look to the shade
It picks out the colours and the light
The prayer. The turning has laid
Darkness to rest. You now take flight

Your heart does not lead you away
It harbours contentment and what is right
The prayer, the knowing has made
Freedom of soul the only fight

The words of wisdom you say
Lift me up to the greatest height
Is prayer the price that I pay?
On my knees I spend the rite

Level in me

Your eyes are dark, deep into which I dive
Reflecting the water in the tears I cried
Oceans of emotion washing in tides
Waves of thirst for you, quench me alive

Flowing fluent in your shining wide sea
Moon sparkle glints on the crests of waves
Lunar light entices, my heart craves
Colourless desire finds it's level in me

Clear yearning finds it's level in me
I am drenched in surging sensation
Drifting soaked in your motioning
Your beckoning tide turns me free

Wide unfathomable mystery
Immerses my spirit, drowns my fears
Sweeps you closer, suffuses you near
With overflow of clarity in destiny

Missing

The hours are long between your song
And hearing silence in the world weigh on

Missing the curl of your smile, an expression
Mile after mile each corner needs turning

Longing bringing longing on so strong
Sorrow yawning rights into wrongs

One heavy sigh more, a second draws
Another and another, deeper than the one before

What was full grows empty so quickly
Darkness envelopes, wraps black around me

Time does not pass by but holds tightly
Strangles patience and spreads it thinly

Motionless, suspended in unyielding ache
Distance stretches further each breath that I take

Healing

Your soul is a clear warm sky
With a sun rising intention
I will never question why

Your heart is a bird in flight
With feathers which catch light
And bright promises in sight

You measure moments with feelings
Truth cannot be denied in time
We draw a long breath, healing

Pauses between your heart beats
Your emotions try to hide
I listen with care, your heart repeats

The truth endures a hue and cry
The truth cries in hues of the sky,
Cerulean cures, upon which we rely

www.ingramcontent.com/pod-product-compliance
Lightning Source LLC
Chambersburg PA
CBHW051753130826
49812CB00033B/1138
* 9 7 8 9 3 9 5 9 5 0 4 6 6 *